JUSTICE SERIES - VOL 3

THE PATH OF
JUSTICE

TAPPING INTO YOUR TREASURES!

STEFFRON T. JAMES

THE PATH OF
JUSTICE

ISBN: 978-0-9998144-6-8
ISBN: 978-0-9998144-7-5 (eBook)

Editor: Tosha Jones of JMC Marketing & Communications (tjones@thejmc.com)
Nashville, Tennessee USA

Content Editor: Debra D. Winans of Linking Solutions LLC (linkingdolutions.net)
Atlanta, Georgia USA

Design & Layout: Michael Matulka of Basik Studios (www.gobasik.com)
Omaha, Nebraska USA

Publisher: Kingdom Living Ministries - Publishing (www.thewayofjustice.com)
Murfreesboro, Tennessee USA

Printed in the United States of America

10 9 8 7 6 5 4 3 2 1

"TRUTH NEVER DAMAGES A CAUSE THAT IS JUST"

- Mahatma Gandhi -

PREFACE
A FRESH PERSPECTIVE ON JUSTICE

"In this booklet, *The Way of Justice*, we will discuss how true justice can help people navigate their way through difficult and tragic situations; we will learn about the correlation between love and justice; we will examine the lives of legendary Bible characters whose just actions paved a way and an example for the people who followed their leadership; and we'll consider how every person can make a difference in someone else's life if he or she is committed to acting in a righteous and just way every day.

THIS IS THE WAY, WALK IN IT

As soon as I sat down in the chair, my barber said, "I have a question for you, pastor." That's the fun title he has coined for me, because every time I come for my bi-monthly hair cut, we get to talk about scripture or an event he's faced from a biblical perspective. He will ask if I can give any insight about a situation he's recently experienced, a Bible verse he's read, a teaching he's heard, a conversation he recently had, or any topic that left him with questions. This has been happening for the better part of two years now.

This particular day, I guess he was anxiously waiting, because he hadn't even wrapped the cape (the wrap placed around my neck to keep hair off my clothes) before he started his inquiry.

"Okay. Let me get settled and fire away," I said. I guess he and one of the other barbers had been discussing the subject and were at an impasse.

"Here it goes," he said. "What is your feeling about prosperity and riches verses staying humble with modest means? A colleague and I were talking about a message we heard where the minister said we should not desire to be rich, but only desire to have sufficient means to stay in a humble place of trusting God!"

Then he finally hit me with the crux of the question: "How do you think God feels about us being rich?"

These types of questions are always loaded. If you give just a canned answer without all the information for the entire situation, then you leave people with a wrong understanding that they apply to a wrong circumstance. Or you could get a bad consequence or apply a misappropriated principle to a circumstance where it does not apply.

That was a mouth full and a great deal to consider. So, my first response to my barber was to get more clarification.

"Are you just talking of God's revealed feelings according to scripture in general regarding us being rich? Or are you talking about a specific instance where God called a person to leave all for a mission He (God) had for the person," I asked? "The two are very different."

"In general," he said. My answer was easy at this point.

I said, "Then I don't have a viewpoint, but I will share a couple of scriptures with you that may give you just a little insight. Are you ready?"

"Yes!" he said.

"Are you sure you're ready?"

He said, "Yes sir."

"This is going to wreck your world for good," I said. "Are you sure you want me to read this?"

I pulled my phone from underneath the cape, unlocked it and went to my ESV (English Standard Version) app. I scrolled to the scripture I wanted and asked one last time, "are you sure?"

I gave the reference and started reading. It was Proverbs 19:4 (ESV) *"Wealth brings many new friends, but a poor man is deserted by his friend."*

His response told the entire story. He said, "Wow! Are you kidding me?"

I said, "No sir. That scripture is in your Bible. And just so you don't think I am pulling one scripture out of thin air, let's go down just to verse seven in the same chapter;

> *7 "All a poor man's brothers hate him; how much more do his friends go far from him! He pursues them with words, but does not have them."*
>
> *- Proverbs 19:7 (ESV)*

After I read the second scripture, I said, "well, what do you think? Does God want you poor? If so, how will you ever win souls if everyone is running from you? If they are deserting you? If they are hating you?"

Of course, the questions were rhetorical and I followed up with two things.

1. God has no problem with poor, He just doesn't want that to be your permanent address.

2. Poverty and poor is a mentality and can give individuals all the excuses needed for not moving beyond their condition.

At that point in the conversation, I felt a need for some balance, so I said, "while I have my phone out and before we get back to my haircut let me read another Proverb to you." This helps prevent people from declaring the rich are evil or there is some type of conspiracy from or for the rich.

According to this verse, just as the poor is made by God, so is the rich. God is the maker of the rich and poor; He causes them to meet together. When the poor meet the rich, he can learn the techniques, principles, disciplines, practices, habits, thoughts, activities, attitudes, and cautions of the rich that have made the rich rich. When the rich meets the poor, he can be exposed to new ways, opportunities, possibilities, shortcuts, procedures, skills, determination, dedication, and faith that are ways of survival that the rich person never imagined or experienced. The poor can become rich or the rich can invest in the capital of the poor. Either way, God can use them right where they are.

"An educated, informed poor man with
a skill may be the richest man alive."

- Steffron James

I then said, "let's get back to my haircut so I can get back to work getting my riches!"

In my thirty plus years in the Lord, twelve years pastoring, thirty years mentoring, conducting Bible studies, business seminars, growth classes, relationship classes, discipleship classes and just conversations at the barber shop, it never fails that sooner or later the question of poor verses rich, poverty verses wealth, haves verses have-nots, abundance verses lack comes up. I am sad to say, rarely do I hear a balanced healthy dialogue ensue. Most fall on polar opposites of the spectrum. Some see it as noble and humble to be poor while they see the rich as pompous and out of touch with God. Then the rich see the poor as ignorant, unintelligent, and uninformed in some critical way that has left them in their current condition.

In this small booklet, I want to up the dialogue to show God is the maker of both rich and poor. Does God give cautions about seeking wealth? You bet! Does he warn the rich to not trust in their riches?

Absolutely! Does he say the **love** of money is the root of all kinds of evil? Yes, and it surely is! But does he tell us that we shouldn't be rich? Never! For the poor, He gives reasons for poverty and then how to turn poverty into wealth and riches. The question is do you believe God and take Him at His word? Or is the rhetoric you have heard about this topic so loud you are entrenched one way or the other? God Himself gives power to get wealth!

> [18] *"You shall remember the LORD your God,*
> *for it is He who gives you power to get wealth,*
> *that He may confirm his covenant that He*
> *swore to your fathers, as it is this day."*
>
> *- Deuteronomy 8:18 (ESV)*

Let's discover this together by slaying the biggest dragon of all, *"the love of money."*

THIS IS THE PATH OF JUSTICE. THIS IS THE WAY, WALK IN IT!

THE PATH OF JUSTICE

INTRODUCTION

A desire. A thirst. A longing for significance. These are the catalysts that have compelled me to write a four-part series about the concept of justice.

Over the past four years, I have been taken to school and to task on this subject that I didn't know had relevance to my purpose or destiny in life. I am a believer in God, but this subject is not limited to, nor exclusive to those of like mind. It is a societal issue and need.

I have discovered that justice may be one of the most misunderstood, but beneficial concepts known to man. However, it may possess the opportunity to right many of the ill we face with humanity. Understanding justice and applying its principles can change governments, countries, cities, individuals, and all in between. It is a way to approach life, other people, situations, and circumstances with balance and soundness.

I know what you are thinking, I must be selling some magic pill or potion. I assure you; I was as shocked as any when I began to realize the implications of this subject. I was even more shocked with the overwhelmingly positive responses I got as I began to share it with others. Individuals who I respect and know to be more studious, well-informed, well-read, contemplative, and honestly smarter than me encouraged me to write this four-part series.

My first book, *Champions of Justice*, was very in-depth and technical. The feedback I received was to present the same information in smaller, bite-sized pieces that are easier to digest and embrace. This would allow those who are newly introduced to the concept of justice to truly grasp its implications and understand its impact.

You are about to eat a small meal that will hopefully keep bringing you back to the table. If you want the full-course meal all at once, you can order *Champions of Justice* from our website: *www.thewayofjustice.com.*

I pray the reading of each book (The Cause of Justice, The Streets of Justice, The Path of Justice, and The Way of Justice) will expose you little-by-little to the relevance and necessity of understanding the concept of justice. These books truly give us a culture-changing perspective of justice.

ENJOY THE APPETIZER!

STEFFRON T. JAMES

THE PATH OF JUSTICE

TABLE OF CONTENT

THE PATH OF JUSTICE

CHAPTER ONE
YOU DON'T LOVE
MONEY ENOUGH

So, it is my time to be all spiritual with God; we do that sometimes. It is the first of the year and I am doing a time of fasting and prayer. I am talking to and praying to God letting Him know how dedicated I am to Him.

I say, "God, Father, I want all you have and all you have prepared for my life." Pretty powerful huh? Then I say, "Father what can I do to honor and serve you more?" I am really on a spiritual roll, aren't I? I finish by saying, "Father, is there anything you would want me to know that will help me please and honor you better? I want to go deeper in you."

I was not prepared for what I heard next. As a matter of fact, I was shocked at what I heard next. Thank God I actually was listening, even if I didn't understand or like what I heard.

As I made my sacrificial statements and waited, I heard almost audibly. He said, *"You can't, you don't love money enough."*

I said, "I rebuke that thought. I take my thoughts captive unto the obedience of Christ." I went back to my spiritual moment and said, "What can I do Father? More time in the Word? More time in prayer? More sacrifices?"

Again, I heard, *"You can't, you don't love money enough."* At this point I became super spiritual and did what Jesus did. I said, "It is written…" and I began to quote every scripture I knew about the love of money, the deceitfulness of riches, and the lust for things. For example, "you'll either love God or money," and "you can't serve two masters."

When I finished my scriptural gymnastics from memory, I had quoted at least ten verses. Long ago, I understood the dangers of riches and money so I wanted to be sure to have my sword of the Word ready should I ever have to slay the money demon if it rose up anytime in me. As I exhausted all my memory scriptures, again I heard, *"You don't love money enough."*

I have been in the Lord a while; I have learned some tricks. If memory verses don't work, I read the scriptures out loud to confirm their reality that it is not my words but God talking. So, I went to 1 Timothy 6:9-10 and read it out loud.

> *9 "But those who desire to be rich fall into temptation, into a snare, into many senseless and harmful desires that plunge people into ruin and destruction. 10 For the love of money is a root of all kinds of evils. It is through this craving that some have wandered away from the faith and pierced themselves with many pangs."*
>
> *- 1 Timothy 6:9-10 (ESV)*

When I finished reading the scripture, this time I heard the voice say again, *"You don't love money enough."* But this time the voice had a sadness. I was arrested by it; I felt the Spirit of God was grieved I wasn't getting this. At that point I felt a pull to read the scripture again. This time I read it slowly and all of a sudden, certain words started leaping off the page at me in bold letters.

Verse nine said, "those who desire to be rich." As I paused, I heard, *"Do you desire to be rich or fulfill my purpose?"* I quickly answered, "I desire to fulfill your purpose."

I continued reading to the end of verse nine. Then I heard, *"If your focus is wrong, then you get wrong results."* I read verse nine again. Then I began to say to myself "if my desire is money, I get temptations, snares, senseless and harmful desires, that plunge people into ruin and destruction."

Right there, I deduced if my desire was to fulfill God's purpose then none of those negative consequences applied! That was tremendous

for me! But verse nine wasn't the showstopper, verse ten was.
So, I slowly began to read verse ten. Again, words began to boldly leap off the page, but it wasn't the first part of the verses "for the love of money is the root of all kinds of evil." It was the *second* part, "it is through this craving that…" Why had I never seen this before? I stopped right at that moment and searched for the definition of the word "craving." Boy was I shocked! It said, "a perverted desire, a sinful longing, lustful intentions, to strive and eagerly long for, and to reach out for in a fleshly way." Another definition said, "a twisted desire."

Right at that moment, I heard the voice again say, *"That is the type of love of money that causes you and any other person issues. But the love of money I long for assigns it, saves it, gives it, sows it, spends it wisely, uses it to advance my kingdom."*

In my stupefied moment I don't know why – other than God's leading – but I started reading again. Seven verses later, I knew why. Paul had just warned a group of people about "the (wrong) kind of love for money," and told them how the desire to be rich can cause damage. He continues addressing them. Take a look at this in your Bible if you have one. In the same breath, in the same section, in the same chapter, he says in verse seventeen,

> *[17] As for the rich in this present age, charge them not to be haughty, nor to set their hopes on the uncertainty of riches, but on God, who richly provides us with everything to enjoy. [18] They are to do good, to be rich in good works, to be generous and ready to share, [19] thus storing up treasure for themselves as a good foundation for the future, so that they may take hold of that which is truly life."*
>
> - 1 Timothy 6:17-19 (ESV)

The rich in this present age; not when Jesus returns, not in the sweet by and by, not any other time besides now. He does not tell them to give away all their wealth. He does not tell them they are unspiritual if they have wealth. He doesn't say they don't love God if they have wealth. All he tells them is to not be haughty, to not trust in the riches but in God, to be ready to do good, and to be generous. In the midst of this, check out the statement, *"God, who richly provides us with everything to enjoy!"*

Are you kidding me? God richly provides the rich everything to enjoy. If this is the case, then why would any of us not choose to be in the camp with this group? Take a look at this next part. When the rich enjoy their riches and use them in the right way they even get a couple of great promises in verse nineteen; *"treasure for a good foundation for the future and the ability to take hold on that which is truly life."* That's in your bible!

Check out this verse:

> [10] *"For to this end we toil and strive,*
> *because we have our hope set on the living*
> *God, who is the Savior of all people,*
> *especially of those who believe."*
>
> *- Timothy 4:10 (ESV)*

Any toiling and striving we do is not to be for riches. Riches are a *byproduct* of setting your hope *on the Rich One!* God knows the heart and the heart's intent. We are to have an end, a resolve, to pursue Him who supplies all of our needs according to His riches in glory (Philippians 4:19). According to His riches, not our goodness. His riches are pretty vast!

I had been robbed. I didn't love money enough to realize God richly provides it for us to enjoy. I simply have to follow His warnings about it and His instructions concerning its use. If God can trust you with the warnings and instructions, then riches are not a problem.

This caused me to earnestly begin to go back to the scriptures and see other things I missed. What else had God said about resources, riches, wealth and abundance? If I had been blind on this basic premise, then what else had I blown past? So, what do the scriptures actually reveal about the poor or poverty which I had seen with a faulty lens?

CHAPTER TWO
HOW POOR ARE WE?

Abject poverty is a part of Africa. There is no way I can teach about riches, wealth, and abundance here. These people don't have the opportunities we have in the United States.

This is a conversation I was having with myself and partly with God as I prepared for a session I would teach the next day. I was in Kenya at the time. I have gone to Kenya sixteen years consecutively. I have seen those getting their meals off the town dump site. I have seen slums so large and vast the number of people in them rival the populations of many of our largest cities. I have seen children, elderly, homeless, widows, orphans, and just humanity so emaciated it is difficult to fathom, and it pains me to witness the depravity.

I hope this isn't offensive, but the U.S. is one of the only countries in the world where you can be poor and still have three meals a day at shelters or helping agencies. Thank God for those who labor in those arenas. Our idea of poverty and that of many third-world countries are light years apart. So how could I dare introduce an American, western culture opportunity of wealth and prosperity to these people? I would be setting them up for pipe dreams, fantasies, wishing on a star, and unachievable desires. So, I decide to play it safe and give them a message about hearing the voice of God.

As I began, the teaching was going really well; I had book, chapter and verse lined up on my iPad and I was just zooming along. There came a point where I needed to do an illustration. I don't know why I did what I did. I was just improvising. I was trying to convey the message that anyone can hear from God.

So, first, I held up the Bible. I was in a church setting so I was pretty safe with my next question. I said as I was holding up the Bible, "Do you here in this room believe this is the Word of God?"

They said, "Yes!"

I said, "Do you believe it is true?"

Again, they said, "Yes." I then said, "Does it work anywhere at any time?" Again, they responded with an emphatic "Yes." Then, to drive my point home, I chose five people from the front row and told them to take their seats, bring them up front, turn them around, face the audience, and sit back in the chairs. I then said, "each of you are going to represent different countries in the world." I went down the line; the U.S., China, Australia, Nigeria, and finally Kenya. Then I stood behind them and began to rehearse the questions I had previously asked, but I asked it about each country. When I got to the last chair which represented Kenya (where we were at the time), I held the Bible over the person's head and said, "Does this Word work in Kenya?"

The crowd may have said yes, but I don't think I heard it. I heard a yes go off in me so loud it drowned out everything else. I realized right in that moment I had limited God, the Word of God, the hand of God...applying only a surface level understanding of God's sovereignty. God's Word works anywhere even when it comes to the elements and promises of wealth, riches, and abundance. I receive a life altering enlightenment right there holding my Bible over the person who represented Kenya. I decided I would never again shy away from teaching what had been revealed to me about wealth and riches because of my audience or location on the planet.

The poor, the impoverished, the destitute, the less fortunate can be a taboo topic. You can talk about helping the poor, reaching out to the poor, providing assistance to the poor, feeding the poor, and aiding the poor. But you better not say the poor have a choice not to be poor. That will get you flogged in many circles and you get accused of being insensitive, high and mighty, calloused, obnoxious, or my favorite, a heel.

Poverty often is a choice and a mentality. Being poor is a season of need which should be in transition. Poverty is your thinking; poor is your condition. Poor is a place of training and preparation. Poverty is a stagnant place of excuses and blame. What do I mean by these statements?

Being poor can happen to anyone. Poor is lack of necessary items, situations, connections, opportunities, resources, or abilities to fully enjoy community and life. Poverty is the lack of will, drive, determination, attitude, and desire to expend the energy to fully enjoy community and life. Poverty keeps you stuck. Poor is just being without what is necessary, now. When I ran across this scripture everything started to make sense to me about the poor.

> [23] *"The fallow ground of the poor would yield much food, but it is swept away through injustice."*
>
> *- Proverbs 13:23*

The fallow ground of the poor would produce much food. That statement was life changing for me. Fallow ground is a field yet to be cultivated. So that means there is a "field of the poor" that if cultivated, has the ability, has the capacity, has the goods to produce **much food**. Look at what this verse uncovers.

The provision in the field of the poor is not just enough to get by and survive; the field of the poor has potential for much. Three words are used to describe this word "much": multitude, abundance, and greatness. The fallow ground, uncultivated field of the poor has multitudes, abundance, and greatness lodged, hidden in what is yet to be seen. But it is being swept away through injustice. That means if we discover any person who is poor or says they are in a poor situation, if we can remove injustice, then the poor produce.

Remember the barber shop story at the beginning? "The rich and poor meet together, the Lord is maker of them both." Poor isn't bad, rich isn't bad; they just have to hook up without injustice. So instead of trying to just give to the poor to increase their poverty, remove injustice and help till their field!

Take a look at a companion scripture to the one I just referenced.

> [13] *"The poor man and the oppressor meet together; the LORD gives light to the eyes of both."*
>
> *- Proverbs 29:13*

Oppressors are the biggest offenders of injustice. But that is not what troubles God. You will always have the poor and you will always have oppressors. But the same Lord gives light to the eyes of **both**. The oppressor is getting his needs met by oppressing. The oppressed, poor, subjected person can get his needs met by learning to use his oppression as a motivator. When he is enlightened about the value in his uncultivated fields, he becomes powerful and invaluable to even the person oppressing.

Let me give an example. Joseph, a familiar character from the Bible, was a slave in Potipher's house. He was poor and Potipher was an oppressor. Joseph was given a light (understanding of what he had that was uncultivated); service! He learned to serve his oppressor faithfully. That light that came from meeting his oppressor led to him presiding over all of Potipher's household.

Shortly after his rise to notability with all those in Potipher's world, he's accused of wrongdoing by Potipher's wife (who lied after Joseph rebuffed her sexual advances) and put in prison. Again, he was placed under an oppressor. But what did he do? Joseph used the light he had again, until he was over everyone in the prison! Finally, when he was brought to Pharaoh, another oppressor, with the light he had, he ended up ruling all of Egypt from a poor and oppressed position.

You can learn from your oppressor. You can rule as an oppressed person and in oppression! Rich and poor, poor and oppressor is not your issue. God made them both. You just need to see right, so your field can be cultivated.

Being a part of the military has been one of the greatest joys of my life. I wouldn't trade my days in blue, US Air Force, for anything. But one of the first things you learn as a new airman in basic training is you no longer have rights. In order for the military to build the type of person who can be a great soldier, the first thing they do is strip you of all identity. Then they use a person who they know you will hate to oppress you into conformity. The best soldiers use this oppression to help unlock their best. Under the severe demands of "rise early, run here, go there, fix this, stop that, correct, adjust, organize, and keep step," the soldiers who persevere and learn the "gold of oppression" are those who are promoted over their peers. All have the same opportunity, but not all advance. Some continued their hate of the oppressor. But for me and others, we learned admiration and appreciation of our oppressor. We gleaned discipline, attention to details, honor, proper submission, team building, doing everything to the best of our ability, and following simple instructions, with much respect. Did we feel oppressed? You bet! But I ask you, reader? Is it about the oppressor; or is it more about how you respond and what you do in your oppression?

Before we examine further the real causes of poverty, let's take a moment to reinforce the plan of God for us to have wealth and riches. I will give a brief commentary after each highlighted scripture.

> [24] "One gives freely, yet grows all the richer; another
> withholds what he should give, and only suffers
> want. [25] Whoever brings blessing will be enriched,
> and one who waters will himself be watered."
>
> - Proverbs 11:24-25

This freely giving is orchestrated, planned, purposeful, second nature giving. It is not just that the person gives, they give with an intention, not to receive but to change the circumstance of others. The unintended consequence is they grow richer as a byproduct. This "grow richer" is an observation of the writer, not the core intention of the giver. These Proverbs are all observations of behavior and the corresponding consequences. Another withholds what should be given, and the consequence is "suffers want." It is not specifically said, but it seems these two individuals have the same or similar opportunities to make a difference.

Somehow, what they have or have received, they know it is not intended for them. However, one gives freely while another withholds. It also doesn't say it here, but there is something going on in the psyche of this individual; a conversation, a contemplation, a choice is made. We will capture some of what might be going on later, but regardless, they withhold and the writer observes the consequence is "suffers want."

Now, look at verse twenty-five. "Whoever brings blessing will be enriched, and one who waters will himself be watered." Not only is this an observation, it is an encouragement, an instruction, a strategy. Bringing blessing means *bringing what will cause another to be fully supplied with what is needed for them to function at full capacity in community.* This person brings what gives another the opportunity to be at full function. What they may need to function is information, a skill, a job opportunity, a different perspective.

Blessing someone can touch the spirit, soul, body, mind, and emotions. Timely and appropriate blessings can completely alter someone's existence. However, it is the bringer of the blessing being enriched, not the receiver (though the receiver can be).

This is a great mystery. You give away, but you become rich. That's mind blowing! Let me make this crystal clear. Blessings may not be resources, riches, or money, though it could be either or all. Realize that plenty of people have money and resources are often miserable. The one who waters will also be watered. Notice the writer never says anything about the receiver of the giving, the blessing, or the watering. Because when it is done with the right intention, regardless of how the recipient responds, whether they are thankful, whether they are appreciative, and whether they receive the benefit is irrelevant. You did your part by what you brought to them. It is their responsibility to appropriately respond and deploy the opportunity.

Sure, there should be an evaluation of where you bring your blessing. Wisdom tells us planting on concrete, a hard heart will not produce. But if we plant in what appears to be good ground and the ground doesn't yield, that does not negate the plan, effort, and investment of the blessing bringer! Let me say this here. You may not believe in God or believe in an accounting for your life when our time on the earth is complete, but I truly believe each person will have to answer for what they willingly brought and what they did with what they receive. We all will give an account.

Now let's get to the "pink elephant" in these two verses. The individual we are to observe becomes richer, is enriched, and is watered. But based on the opening chapter, the philosophy and thinking of many would be, "this person should be rejecting of these three things." I believe the problem isn't having money, but not knowing what to *do* with the money we have. Because according to these two verses, we should never be lacking.

I will give you two thoughts to consider on this next exploration.

⁴ "The reward for humility and fear of the LORD is riches and honor and life."

- Proverbs 22:4

¹⁶ "Long life is in her right hand; in her left hand are riches and honor."

- Proverbs 3:16

The first verse encourages a character trait of humility and a disposition to fear the Lord. The writer sees these two things as necessary ingredients for what is called a reward. The combined effect of these two essentials is threefold:

1. Riches

2. Honor

3. Life

Let me unfold this a bit if I may.

If we believe riches are a detriment to us, if we believe the evils of them will ultimately lead us astray, then we believe the risks outweigh the rewards. We believe the only way to stay free from the entanglements of the cares of this world, the deceitfulness of riches, and the lust for things is to stay **humble** and without an observation of this scripture reveals the same humility you want to embrace when coupled with the fear (reverence) for God (who and what He is) **brings riches**.

I want you to get this, so let's pace ourselves. *Humility and reverence equal riches.* So, the only thing that results in not bringing riches is if you are missing one of these two ingredients! Either you are **not** being humble or **not** fearing God? If the Word we quote is true, then we have a dilemma. Because when you combine the two, humility and reverence for God, you get a reward of riches, honor, and life (fullness of life). Check your ingredients. True humility and true reverence bring riches, honor, and life! Shocking I know; this blew me away, too!

The second verse comes in the middle of a commentary on wisdom by the writer. We are always encouraged to get wisdom, embrace wisdom, seek wisdom, invite wisdom, give wisdom first place...we are even told wisdom is the principle thing we should desire. Again, we have a dilemma. When wisdom shows up, it holds out both of its hands which become *your* hands when *you* embrace wisdom. Here's the quandary: an observation of the scripture says in wisdom's right hand is long life and in wisdom's left hand are riches and honor. Do we want wisdom? Then how can we deny what comes with it – long life, riches, and honor?

This is a good place to stop and ponder. Have you limited God as I had? I had to repent and ask God to show me His truth about wealth because I was missing it. The scripture says, "God's people perish for a lack of knowledge." My desire is nothing perishes that could have been yours or mine.

Ready to do some more digging? I thought so!

> [11] **"Whoever** works his land will have plenty of bread,
> but he who follows worthless pursuits lacks sense."
>
> - Proverbs 12:11

"Whoever?" Rich, poor, economically challenged, oppressed, widow, orphan, homeless, disenfranchised, discriminated against, born in poverty, born on the wrong side of the tracks, and the like.

"Works his land?" All of us have been given this extraordinary gift called life. Each of us have a little piece of dirt on the earth that is full of potential; ideas, imaginations, thoughts, drive, vision, creative insights, skill, strength, ability, and energy, just to name a few. According to an observation of this scripture, if we work what we have – though we may have nothing externally provided to us – then we actually have plenty of bread potential. Notice it didn't say just enough to survive!

In biblical times, if someone had plenty of bread, then it was a sign of prosperity. People who use their potential in their little piece of dirt can have plenty. But there is a but! "He who follows worthless pursuits lacks sense." If you take your strength, ability, and energy and waste them on pursuing worthless (empty, vain, leading to trouble, no benefit, frivolous) things, then good and common sense has left the building. Steffron didn't say it, the text did!

YOU CAN'T PURSUE WORTHLESSNESS AND GET WORTH. BUT THOSE WHO WORK WHAT THEY HAVE GET WORTH OUT OF THEMSELVES.

There are individuals in life who can't work due to injury, birth defects, handicaps, mental incapacitation, and other ailments. These individuals become opportunities for others to bring blessing and water. So even if some are truly unable to fully contribute to community, they give justice opportunities, employment, and areas of creativity, as they learn how to help these individuals function. Some great inventions were the result of trying to address a handicap. The incapacitated enrich justice providers with opportunities to be selfless, distribute, and build character. Both groups are a vital part of the community. Here's the amazing thing; the bringers of blessing to the less fortunate get enriched as they enrich!

Before I go to the companion scripture of Proverbs 12:11, let's take a quick detour to reinforce my just mentioned commentary.

> [23] "In all toil/work/labor (depending on the translation, these three words are used) there is profit, but mere talk tends only to poverty."
>
> - Proverbs 14:23

In **all** toil/work/labor there is a profit! Even if it is not seen at first. We work for a week or month before we get paid. Your work pays. But the work is always first. Preparation is never wasted time. If you work your land, then it will pay off.

I worked for this lady once when I was a little boy. I had a certain item I wanted to buy and my parents didn't have or wouldn't give me the money. I don't even recall what it was at this time. But I wanted it so bad I was willing to work for it. So, I asked permission to go to all the neighbors and see if I could find work. With my mother's permission, off I went the next morning.

Several places I stopped had nothing. But then I got to Mrs. Betty Richardson's house. I knocked on the door, used my most pleasant tone, and minded all the manners my mother had taught me. For example, I addressed Mrs. Richardson as "Ma'am." My mother taught me to say ma'am and sir to anyone older than me. And if we ever omitted it within earshot of her, then an immediate corrective pop or pinch quickly followed.

"Ma'am," I said to Mrs. Richardson. "I wonder if you might have some chores or work, I could do for you. I am trying to make a little extra money."

Mrs. Richardson smiled big and said, "that is just so wonderful, young-uns don't want to work for anything now a days." That's how they talk where I am from in Liberty Hill, South Carolina. "Sure, I have some work you can do," she continued. "I have been needing to rake up the leaves in this yard for weeks, but I just can't seem to get around to it. If you rake them up in piles and dump them in one location, I will be happy to pay you."

At that point I turned around and surveyed the yard. It was an old plantation house with massive oaks all throughout the yard. But I had asked for work, so here it went.

I raked from ten in the morning until after three in the afternoon. Finally, I finished and knocked on the door announcing my completion. When Mrs. Richardson came to the door, she looked over my shoulder and said, "Well done young man, you seem to have done an excellent job. My mother always taught me, whatever you do, do it to the best of your ability. Let me go get your pay."

It was a grueling afternoon. It was hot, the leaves were dusty, and I was filthy from head to toe, but it was worth it. I would be able to buy my much-desired item. When Mrs. Richardson returned, she handed me one dollar and fifty cents and an apple. She thanked me and off she went back into the house. On my way home, I bit into the apple and it was half rotten. I was so angry, I cried halfway home.

My labor had made me a profit, a whole buck fifty. But there was another value I receive at the age of nine. Always negotiate your pay **before** you do the work. Mrs. Richardson had taught me a valuable life lesson that would help me tremendously in the future.

In all labor there is profit, even if not what you originally think it might be. At times, the value and profit of your work is more about what you learned, then what you tangibly receive in payment. Work is your revealer! It reveals your gifts and abilities. It reveals your passions. It reveals your strengths and weaknesses. It reveals your ignorance and knowledge. Work reveals you!

Get to know how a person works and you get to know the person. By the way, yes, when she went back inside the house, I thought seriously about spreading the leaves all over the yard again, but I was too tired!

Now the companion to Proverbs 12:11:

> [19] *"Whoever works his land will have plenty of bread, but he who follows worthless pursuits will have plenty of poverty.* [20] *A faithful man will abound with blessings, but whoever hastens to be rich will not go unpunished.* [21] *To show partiality is not good, but for a piece of bread a man will do wrong.* [22] *A stingy man hastens after wealth and does not know that poverty will come upon him"*
>
> *- Proverbs 28:19-22*

This first verse sets up the same as our previous one, but gives a different conclusion. In 12:11 the person who follows worthless pursuits "lacks sense." In this section, the person will have plenty of poverty, plenty of what they already have. So, if you use your potential on the wrong endeavors called worthless, then you are guaranteed two things: you have no sense and plenty of poverty.

However, this section doesn't stop there. It goes on to say in verse twenty, "a faithful man or human or woman."

Faithful means reliable, trustworthy, consistent, firm, steady, fidelity, and having integrity. This person will abound (multiply greatly) with blessings; but whoever hastens to be rich will not go unpunished. Notice the writer had no problem with the individual abounding in full supply in every way. But the writer quickly gives the instruction and warning of what to avoid, which is, trying to find a get rich quick scheme. That person experiences punishment. But the faithful is abounding.

Then he shows one of the ways you can potentially hasten after riches, showing partiality. Look at what it says; for a **piece** of bread the person does wrong. In our previous verse, just working your land brought about plenty of bread. Now for a single piece of bread those who want riches without faithfulness will do wrong.

The last verse gives the actual description for this person. The verse calls the person "stingy." It is a stingy person who runs quickly after wealth! He pursues get rich quick schemes and shows partiality. This is why the "worthless pursuit followers" lack sense. They don't know they are actually inviting poverty. Wow, that's me responding!

> [4] *"The soul of the sluggard craves and gets nothing, while the soul of the diligent is richly supplied."*
>
> *- Proverbs 13:4*

A sluggard is a lazy person. The one who is unwilling to expend the energy to do what is needed: to work, be faithful, reliable, consistent, trustworthy, firm, or skilled at a valued commodity. But get this, a sluggard craves everything! He has no shortage of desire, dreams, and aspirations; but sadly, he gets nothing because he is a slug. At the same the time, *while* this person is being lazy, another person with the *same* opportunity is being diligent and is getting *richly supplied.* What is the difference between these two and the poverty path? Choice! We begin to see, lazy verses diligent, quick verses steady, and worthless pursuits verses work.

THE INGREDIENTS DETERMINE THE OUTCOME.

[24] *"The hand of the diligent will rule,*
while the slothful will be put to forced labor."

- Proverbs 12:24

Here is that word *diligent* again. "The hand" speaks of the things *you do.* Your interactions with your environment and people. If you are diligent (persevere, don't quit, don't give up), then you end up ruling.

I need to clarify here. The word "rule" is better translated, "to master." It is not about mastering or ruling a person or other people. It is mastering a task, function, skill, idea, a thing that makes you the expert or person of need. When you are the person who has mastered, you are called upon to teach, share, and transfer that knowledge and skill to others. You can also be paid for your mastery. At the same time, another individual with the same opportunity is slothful (lazy) and is put to forced labor because he didn't choose to labor.

Here is the hidden truth. You will end up working either way; the choice is whether you benefit greatly from your labor or others as they guide you to do what they mastered. You get paid, but they receive the larger payoff and benefits. Those who have mastered make the rules.

This element has to do with developing a competence as a person. It is developing your value and worth to society.

IF YOU HAVE NOTHING TO OFFER OF VALUE; YOU WILL BE OFFERED NOTHING OF VALUE!

Your worth to others is commensurate with the value of what you bring! Though as a person you are a treasure, that treasure has to be mined out of you for beneficial use. Gold in the ground has great worth, but until it is mined, its value is unknown.

> [17] *"Whoever is generous to the poor lends to*
> *the LORD, and he will repay him for his deed."*
>
> *- Proverbs 19:17*

In response to this scripture, I want to ask a couple of questions.

- Question one: How can you be generous if you don't have enough to be generous with?

- Question two: How can you be the generous and the poor at the same time?

- Question three: The writer of this verse seems to indicate the generous person is lending to the Lord. So, am I wrong to suppose this person is closer to God than the poor person?

- Question four: God will repay the generous to the poor, who are actually lending to the Lord. What if the generous person who is lending to the Lord is rich?

- Question five: If they are rich and God repays them, won't that make them at least as rich or richer?

- Question six: If God has a problem with you being rich, wouldn't this all violate His own truth of how He feels?

- Question seven: When you read this verse, do you see yourself as the generous person or the poor person?

"Whoever" means God made both rich and poor and everything in between. Those who are considered poor by one standard in the U.S. can be a blessing to another in a third-world country who sees them as rich. Poor and rich are relative.

> [15] *"Slothfulness casts into a deep sleep,*
> *and an idle person will suffer hunger."*
>
> *- Proverbs 19:15*

You get it. No need to beat you over the head.

[4] *"The sluggard does not plow in the autumn;
he will seek at harvest and have nothing."*

- Proverbs 20:4 (ESV)

Let me dig a little deeper for a moment from my personal experience on plowing and laziness. We don't plow anymore, at least many of us don't. I sure had my share as a kid and an adult. It was grandma who always wanted the garden. We wanted what the garden produced, but the early mornings when you were off for the summer or on an early Saturday morning on the weekend, the last thing you wanted to hear was, "Get up! It is time to go to the garden."

But the reward came in the winter. I recall days it would snow. We lived twenty-one miles to the closest town. If it snowed, then you couldn't drive on the roads and often the power would go out. Getting food at the store was impossible. Of course, us kids would wonder what we were going to do. Grandma would go back to the back bedroom and come out with jars. There was soup, vegetables, preserves and all kinds of goodies.

"Where did these come from," we would ask?

"Remember the garden," Grandma responded? "We put some of the harvest up for rainy and snowy days. Because we plowed in the summer we have now."

If we would be honest, much of our lack is due to not plowing. Plowing indicates preparation for a future harvest. Several things have to be done for this future harvest. First, there is the tilling of the land. This is done long before a harvest is expected. This tilling can be hard labor depending on if the soil has ever been plowed. Weeds, trees, rocks, and other items may have to be removed in order to till the land. Once the land is tilled, then it can be plowed.

Plowing is where order is laid out for your intended harvest. In a garden, plowing lays out rows for the different crops you want to have come in. In our day and age, it's referred to as investment, education, work, real estate, bonds, annuities, IRAs, etc. These are modern day plowings and tilling, preparation for harvest. You layout what you want to produce at harvest.

The last thing you must do is plant the seed. Here is what is so interesting.

THE SEED NEVER LOOKS LIKE WHAT IT PRODUCES AT HARVEST, BUT WITHOUT IT THERE WILL BE NO HARVEST.

Depending on the seed, it may take some time for it to come up. When it does, it still does not look like what it is going to be. Think of any fruit or vegetable; the first thing you see is not the fruit, but a green twig or vine. It is only after we've worked the process that we get to enjoy the fruits of our front-end labor. However, if you have planted nothing, why are you seeking at harvest? The writer states the obvious, you "have nothing." There is always a system, process, and method to harvest.

I want to wrap up in a tight little bow for you this section and these scriptures on poverty, the poor, the rich, the wealthy, and everything in between. The scripture definitely gives us cautions and instructions about the dangers of riches. But the scriptures are no less explicit when giving the dangers and cautions about being poor or having a poverty mentality. Here we go.

CHAPTER THREE
THE SYSTEM TO HARVEST

"A slack hand causes poverty,
but the hand of the diligent makes rich."

- Proverbs 10:4

Look what the writer says is the culprit for poverty; a slack hand. It is not where you were born, who oppresses or oppressed you. It is not because someone didn't give you a chance. It is not because of the color of your skin. It is not even misfortune. There's that "but" in the verse.

The antithesis of having a slack hand is having a "diligent hand." And a diligent hand has a result; it makes rich. To make it as plain as possible: if you aren't becoming rich or richer, then you are possibly dealing with a slack hand in your affairs and need to apply another level of diligence.

Listen, rich is in the eye of the beholder. To the person who has only seen one, a hundred dollars might appear rich. For the person who has seen a thousand, ten thousand may be rich. For the person who has seen a million, a billion may be rich. And for a person who has never known family and peace, to have them may be rich and worth more than all the money and resources in the world. Either way, the result of the diligent is rich. This is written for each of us to know, understand, and embrace as we learn through scripture.

15 *"A rich man's wealth is his strong city;*
the poverty of the poor is their ruin."

- Proverbs 10:15

Warning: don't make the wealth you have your confidence and thing you trust in for your future. Don't make wealth the focus. A strong city that was considered impenetrable, it gave protection from defeat, insulated those inside from the outside world, and strong cities were paramount to survival. The caution is to not trust the wealth.

Second Warning: the poverty the poor are experiencing can be their ruin. It can destroy them. The poor's perception of their poverty is more dangerous than the poverty. If the poverty people are experiencing results in them feeling entitled because of their suffering, dependent on another for their future, reliant on programs, aids, or assistance as a means of continued life, if they stop looking to be a contributor to society and only look to receive, then their poverty has ruined them. People with a poverty mindset see no solutions coming from inside them, but completely outside of them. Is there assistance needed at times when life has tragically fallen apart and all is in shambles? Absolutely! But it should be temporary and short term to allow the person to stabilize and get proper footing to reengage in the community.

> [13] *"Love not sleep, lest you come to poverty;*
> *open your eyes, and you will have plenty of bread."*
>
> *- Proverbs 20:13*

Have you noticed a pattern yet? The writer of these proverbs doesn't make the poor victims. The difficulty of being poor, oppressed and in poverty is not dismissed; but the responsibility for departing poverty is placed squarely on the shoulders of the person who is poor. I feel this is where we have had a breakdown in our efforts towards the poor. We have felt sorry for them, but haven't felt bad enough in some cases to let our bad feeling initiate helping get them back into community. We also have felt so sorry for them that we don't allow them to feel the pain of poor enough to want to expend whatever energy necessary to leave the state of being poor.

> [26] *"A worker's appetite works for him;*
> *his mouth urges him on."*
>
> *- Proverbs 16:26*

If you haven't liked some of these scriptures, you really won't like this one!

*⁷ "The rich rules over the poor, and the borrower is
the slave of the lender."*

- Proverbs 22:7

Here's my question. When you read this verse, do you see yourself as, the rich or the poor person, the borrower or the lender? How you see yourself is one hundred percent reality for you. Even, if it is not totally true or only true temporarily.

One more question: if you are a person who believes in God, which position do you think God would prefer you to occupy? Would He want you to be able to help, bring a right attitude, a right grace, an esteeming demeanor, fair and honest terms to dealings with the poor and borrower? I say this is the place God has desired for His people from the beginning. Genesis chapter one, says, "be fruitful, multiply, subdue, have dominion, rule on the earth." Make it better, bring out its best, your best! Being rich and richly supplying has been the assignment from the beginning. How can we be in the image and likeness of God and not be rich? Just asking. Don't shoot me down! Each of us is given time and opportunity. Even if the opportunity has unfairness, oppression, difficulty, and hardship. We get to choose what we do with the hand we're dealt.

I didn't know my paternal grandfather well. He died when I was less than a year old. But somehow, I remember him. He grew up in the early nineteen hundred's when blacks were still severely oppressed, and in the back woods of South Carolina, prejudice and racism were alive and well. But the stories I heard about my grandfather described him as a hard worker and great at negotiating. He worked on a farm for one of the plantation owners. He helped make the man he worked for successful. After years of working for him, he came to the man and told him he wanted land of his own. He had six children and wanted them to have it better than he did. He agreed to a certain number of years of working (I am not sure there was any pay involved) and he received sixty-six acres. That sixty-six acres is still in the family as a result of my grandfather's labor. In all labor there is profit. We just have to prepare for what we want to come!

He that works his land will have plenty of bread and land. My grandfather didn't make excuses for the situation he was handed;

he made something of it. Each of us can use what we have! Even though I didn't know my grandfather, I now have as a part of my inheritance a fruit of his labor. What you work and long for may be the encouragement and source of inspiration for those generations following you.

> [22] "A good man leaves an inheritance
> to his children's children, but the sinner's
> wealth is laid up for the righteous."
>
> - Proverbs 13:22 (ESV)

I believe my grandfather was a good man. According to this scripture he at least met one of the criteria. Are you a good person? Do you have it in your thinking to leave an inheritance? If the sinner's wealth is laid up for the righteous and you consider yourself righteous, are you turning down what should be yours? Or should I say, what should be your children's children's? We have failed our coming generations by not preparing for them. Thank God my grandfather did! Now, the question is will I? I must.

This next scripture out of 2 Corinthians 9 is a bit longer to read, but because it is one of the most misused and misapplied, I would be remiss if I didn't address it. First of all, if you start at verse one, then you find the Apostle Paul is encouraging the believers in the region of Achaia, better known as the Corinthians, to have their gift or offering ready for the poor in Judea. It was a gift the people of Achaia had earlier willingly promised to send. Paul had been bragging about them in Macedonia, so he was telling them to please be prepared in case some of the people of Macedonia were with him when he arrives to collect the gift. Paul could end up being embarrassed for bragging on them.

This is the backdrop to verse six that we have been hearing preached in offering services, giving campaigns, appreciations, anniversaries, building funds, and even for the pastor's new car or plane. It is one of the favorites for the weekly tithes and offerings also. But in context, verse six has nothing to do with any of those things. Therefore, any promises or instructions associated with this text may not be applicable either. One last thing, in verse five, Paul cautions that this is a gift they promised and is in no way an extraction. Let's read from verse six.

> [6] *"The point is this: whoever sows sparingly will also reap sparingly, and whoever sows bountifully will reap bountifully. [7] Each one must give as he has decided in his heart, not reluctantly or under compulsion, for God loves a cheerful giver. [8] And God is able to make all grace abound to you, so that having all sufficiency in all things at all times, you may abound in every good work. [9] As it is written, "He has distributed freely, he has given to the poor; his righteousness endures forever."*
>
> *- 2 Corinthians 9:6-9*

The point is this. Who is he talking to? Those who have previously made the promise to give. He is not talking to a new group. He is not talking to everyone in Achaia. He is not even talking to the entire church. He is speaking to those who made a commitment and now it is time to follow through on the commitment they made of their own volition.

Perhaps in good faith, they made the commitment and after some time, life occurred and they spent the money or the strength of their desire to give lost its intensity. They may not be as impassioned as when the promise was initially made. We must understand Paul is speaking to a specific identified group. If we miss that one key factor, then this becomes a scripture to guilt people into giving.

The proper insight shown in context reveals the legitimate, applicable, and befitting way to use this scripture requires the individuals to have previously – from their own free will – promised to supply a specific thing. It has to be a person making a vow with no pressure applied. After their unpressured open commitment, people should be able to reasonably expect their compliance to their promise.

Verse seven is the verse I think we should lead with any time we quote this scripture. It says, "Each one must give as he has decided in his heart, not reluctantly or under compulsion." The last part says, "for God loves a cheerful giver." Who's a cheerful giver? The person not giving reluctantly or under compulsion. If there is any arm twisting, emotional manipulating, guilt-inciting pleas for money, then this scripture is violated. Oh, just for good measure, the request for money is for the poor, not for the daily needs of the ministry. Worth considering isn't it?

If I am not reading or comprehending this passage in context, please show me what you see; I'm open. Verses eight and nine are associated with those who keep their promise, "they give to the poor, and sow bountifully." He is telling them they can trust God if they supply the lack of others and distribute freely.

> [17] *"He that lends to the poor lend to the Lord and the Lord will repay."*
>
> *- Proverb 19:17*

The mirror of that verse in the New Testament is in the next part of our Corinthian's text.

> [8] *"God is able to make **all grace** abound towards you, that you will have all sufficiency in everything and be able to abound in every good work."*
>
> *- 2 Corinthians 9:8*

That is a mouth full. But God is making a promise to those who promised to supply to the poor. Here's the snapshot; you supply to others what you have promised and you will never lack. God will give you more than you can imagine so you can keep on supplying!

This is where I get in trouble. If your sacrifice is not for the poor, then is God obligated to repay you? Inquiring minds want to know! Be careful of what gets spun as providing for the poor. Let me give you a little litmus test. Notice the people of Achaia had previously been moved to send aid. Paul was simply reminding them.

1. What do you already have in your heart to do to help the poor?

2. If you hear of a need for the poor, your heart is pricked, you are drawn to supply without compulsion and you feel no reluctance, then by all means give.

3. Do you have to violate a previous instruction, vow, commitment, wisdom, or sound principle? If you do, then you may want to get counsel on the idea.

As it is written:

> *⁹ "He has distributed freely, he has given to the poor; his righteousness endures forever."*
>
> *- Psalms 112:9*

The promise is to those who distribute freely to the poor. Again, for those who have a problem with being rich, how can you distribute what you don't have? I won't break down the rest of this though it is really good. For the sake of time, read the parts I put in bold.

Starting with verse ten:

> *¹⁰ "He who supplies seed to the sower and bread for food will supply and multiply your seed for sowing and increase the harvest of your righteousness. ¹¹ **You will be enriched in every way** to be generous in every way, which through us will produce thanksgiving to God. ¹² For the ministry of this service is **not only supplying the needs of the saints but is also overflowing in many thanksgivings to God.** ¹³ By their approval of this service, they will glorify God because of your submission that comes from your confession of the gospel of Christ, and **the generosity of your contribution for them and for all others,** ¹⁴ while they long for you and pray for you, because of the surpassing grace of God upon you. ¹⁵ **Thanks be to God for his inexpressible gift!"***
>
> *- 2 Corinthians 2:10-15*

What is the inexpressible gift? You and I being suppliers for the needs of others at God's direction with the very resources and increases provided by Him through us to others. Did you get that? When God can trust you to get His resources to others, He keeps on giving to you and through you. But in the end, you have much bread!

THE PATH OF JUSTICE

CHAPTER FOUR
WHAT IS "THIS THING?"

¹¹ *"Then God said to him: "Because you have asked this thing, and have not asked long life for yourself, nor have asked riches for yourself, nor have asked the life of your enemies, but have asked for yourself understanding to discern justice,* ¹² *behold, I have done according to your words; see, I have given you a wise and understanding heart, so that there has not been anyone like you before you, nor shall any like you arise after you.* ¹³ *And I have also given you what you have not asked: both riches and honor, so that there shall not be anyone like you among the kings all your days."*

- 1 Kings 3:11-13 (NKJV)

This story is about King Solomon, the son of King David. David had been a mighty warrior and conqueror who led his people and established an unparalleled kingdom for the time. Solomon is taking over and wants to ensure he honors his father's legacy. David had tremendously relied on the God of Abraham, Isaac, and Jacob as he ruled. Solomon saw it as important to at least acknowledged the God of his father. Shortly after taking the throne, Solomon prays a prayer to the God of his father. What you read in the above verses is God's reply to the new king.

Verse eleven, "Then God said to him, because you have asked this thing." What is "this thing?" The text talks quickly about things he could have asked or requested but chose not to. Notice asking for riches is in the list of nots, along with long life, or wanting your enemies dead. Here comes the thing, "but have asked for yourself understanding to discern justice." This is the thing that unlocks, releases, affords, taps into all that comes next.

This God of David begins by saying, "I have given you a wise and understanding heart." In other words, a heart of justice is a wise and understanding heart. The byproduct of justice is wisdom and a true understanding of affairs. Now comes the crazy part, because he asked for what God calls "this thing."

We can assume it is the "right thing," "best thing," "appropriate thing," and the "needed thing." Then it is declared by God, no one before or after him would be like him. Here comes that gravy in verse thirteen. God says because of this thing, "I have given you what you have not asked; both riches and honor, so that there shall not be anyone like you among the kings all your days."

Much of what we have been exploring in this book is a result of Solomon's writings. I can confidently say there has not arisen in the annals of history a king like Solomon. His wisdom and the wealth he amassed are unrivaled. If God had a problem with riches, then he blew it with this king. Riches weren't Solomon's undoing. It was insecurity and women. Have you ever asked for a heart to discern justice? This is what opened up everything for Solomon. What will open up things for your legacy?

I believe this interaction of King Solomon with the God of his father, David, gives us a glimpse into something which is a crucial component of any discussion of riches, wealth, poverty, governing people or life. Before we close out this brief look at Solomon, I want you take a look at what was a key part of why the Bible has the book of Proverbs.

> [1] *"The proverbs of Solomon, son of David, king of Israel:* [2] *To know wisdom and instruction, to understand words of insight,* [3] **to receive instruction in wise dealing, in righteousness, justice, and equity;"**
>
> *- Proverbs 1:1-3*

One of the first mentioned reasons for Proverbs to be penned is righteousness, justice, and equity. We have heard a great deal about righteousness and we should. We have heard a great deal about equity, also. But I know for me until a couple of years ago, justice was nowhere on my radar. It wasn't even in my zip code. But according to the man who was considered as wise as any, instruction in wise dealings flows out of an understanding of all three, not just the two you are familiar with. Lastly, Proverbs 28:5 (ESV) says, *"Evil men do not understand justice, but those who seek the LORD understand it completely."*

UNDERSTANDING JUSTICE COMPLETELY IS ESSENTIAL TO DEALING WISELY IN LIFE.

Solomon was rich. He was wise. God spoke to Him on at least two occasions. He was used by God. God never seemed to have a concern with him being rich. God's instructions to Solomon revolved around dealing wisely with righteousness, justice, and equity. Solomon is an Old Testament personality and many may dismiss his significance because it is not a part of the New Covenant. I would like to now take you to my new, New Testament hero. We find in this person many of the characteristics God was looking for and instructing for Solomon. Take a look at my new hero Zacchaeus. This hero also had a conversation with God.

If you're interested, you can read where I go into much detail in my book *Champions of Justice*. But for the sake of time, I won't go in depth here; however, I surely want you to get the takeaway of how essential this story is to our subject matter.

I am fascinated by this man, who he was, and his conversation with Jesus. Check it out with me in Luke 19:1-10. Jesus spends the afternoon with a rich guy named Zacchaeus. No big deal, right? Except, this is the last person He interacts with before going into Jerusalem to die. Except, He leaves in the middle of the road an entire entourage of disciples, followers, the no longer blind Bartimaeus, all who came with Him from Galilee, the people of Jericho who lined the streets, and everyone who He picked up on the way to His triumphal entry to Jerusalem. He leaves them and goes to lunch with a short man who just climbed down out of the tree.

What was it about this man that caused Jesus to esteem and elevate him to such an honored status? Earlier in Jesus' trip, He had declined to delay His journey to Jerusalem for the Samaritans, an entire town. And now He was taking a detour for one man. Much has been said about this man, but let me give you a few highlights I have observed for your consideration. Here are my Zacchaeus callouts: He was a chief tax collector, so he was in a place of rule and influence. He was an everyday working class "Joe" who had built a successful business. He was a rich man. Now, the text does not say how he became rich. But since it says chief, it would imply there was a time he was not, a time when he had an entry level position. Perhaps he applied the verses we reviewed above!

> [4] "The reward for humility and fear of the LORD is riches and honor and life"
>
> - Proverbs 22:4

> [24] "One gives freely, yet grows all the richer; another withholds what he should give, and only suffers want. [25] Whoever brings blessing will be enriched, and one who waters will himself be watered."
>
> - Proverbs 11:24-25

This is totally my conjecture. However, something happened to bring him to become rich and something happened for Jesus to take time for just this man.

Much like many of us, Zacchaeus was seeking Jesus out. But on account of the size of the crowd, he couldn't even get close enough to see this guy he'd heard about. This tells us just how large the crowd was, just in Jericho. Another observation, though Zacchaeus was a chief tax collector and rich, the people of Jericho didn't seem intimidated by him. They didn't move out of the way and give him a place at the front of the crowd. One other thing along these lines, Zacchaeus didn't have an entourage surrounding him though he was rich. Most rich guys would travel with servants or guards to ensure their safety or to keep beggars from approaching them. They also would probably have someone else climb a tree for them. As I read the text, I felt it showed a man with a certain level of humility or at least a person who isn't flashy with the trapping of his wealth.

Let's keep moving with our callouts in the next part of the story. Zacchaeus, who's apparently five foot nothing, is up in the tree positioned to see the man from Galilee. Jesus comes straight to the tree where Zacchaeus has perched himself. Take a look at verse five.

> [5] *"And when Jesus came to the place, he looked up and said to him, 'Zacchaeus, hurry and come down, for I must stay at your house today."*
>
> *- Luke 19:5*

Here is my conjecture again, "if you are the right type of person, God can lead you up in a tree and come find you in the same tree." God sees you in your lowest or highest place. Zacchaeus had to get up in the tree to see Jesus, he didn't have to be in the tree for Jesus to see him!

As an example, a woman with a blood disease came up behind him in a huge crowd and touched Jesus at one point in His travels. He felt the virtue go out of Him and He said, "who touched me?" He hadn't known she was there; but knew she touched him.

I submit for your consideration that Jesus knew of Zacchaeus before he ever came to Jericho, before he ever climbed up in the tree. How do I deduce this? From the statement, "for I must stay at your house today." Jesus knew he had a house. Let's consider this while we are using our imaginations.

He said, "I *must*." That sounds like an assignment to me. Jesus didn't say, *would it be okay, if you are prepared, if you can receive me, if your house is not too far, not even, if you have a house?* This guy has Jesus' attention, heaven's attention, everyone from Jericho's attention, and the attention of everyone on the journey from Galilee. I ask, "who is this guy and why him?"

> 6 *"So [Zacchaeus] hurried and came*
> *down and received [Jesus] joyfully."*
>
> *- Luke 19:6*

For the sake of time, I won't jump heavily into this, but Jesus told him to hurry and come down. And this verse says he "hurried."

OBEYING DIVINE INSTRUCTIONS QUICKLY IS A PRINCIPLE THAT YIELDS AMAZING BENEFITS.

Next it said, "he receives Jesus joyfully." That also is a divine principle that yields amazing benefits. Quick obedience with joy is a kingdom key for unlocking doors you never imagined would open for you— that was a freebie!

Verse seven says, "And when they saw it, they all grumbled, 'He has gone in to be the guest of a man who is a sinner'." A couple of things to draw from this statement. It could not have been the disciples or the people on the journey with Jesus who said this; they didn't know Zacchaeus. I deduce this statement being made caused all who were traveling with Jesus to look directly at Jesus for clarification, confirmation, or denial. What had they seen? Jesus inviting himself to this guy's house, who Jesus calls by name. The people of Jericho grumble and say, "[Jesus] has gone to be the guest," which is an accusation or an indictment against Jesus first.

Then there is an accusation against Zacchaeus, "a man who is a sinner." Let's get the scene. Jesus and Zacchaeus have turned to walk away ("gone") with no explanation, with no invitation for anyone to join them, with seemingly no consideration of all who had come with him and no regard to all who had come out to see him. Jesus leaves them all and begins to walk off with Zacchaeus. Obviously, the grumbles and accusations are loud enough to be heard by Jesus and Zacchaeus.

Let's unpack verse eight with its callouts. "And Zacchaeus stood and said to the Lord, "Behold, Lord, the half of my goods I give to the poor. And if I have defrauded anyone of anything, I restore it fourfold."

"Lord, behold Lord." This acknowledgement is pretty powerful. At no time did the text say Jesus was anything more than a man Zacchaeus wanted to see. He possibly had heard of the miracles performed, the healings, the fish and loaves, and just before Jesus reached Zacchaeus' tree, a blind man is healed. Yet without any other knowledge about Jesus that's revealed by the text, he calls Him Lord, twice! I coin it the tree conversion (you will know a tree by the fruit it bears). Zacchaeus went up in a tree to see a man and came down knowing a Lord.

Get this, twice he said, "Lord," as if the first time didn't quite capture the reverence he intended. Somewhere between going up in the tree and being called a sinner, Zacchaeus realized this was more than just a man who did miracles. This man wasn't the typical. He was Lord! Perhaps it was because Jesus had called him by name.

If you did a study of the culture of that time, you'd discover for someone to call another person Lord was monumental. Zacchaeus was saying, "I see you, Jesus, as the owner of everything, even me!" I believe this next part of what Zacchaeus said was also directed toward Jesus, because as Lord (owner), He would be the only person who knew if this next statement was true.

Jesus and Zacchaeus stop. Everyone is looking at Jesus. With this newfound revelation from the grumbling crowd that this man is a sinner, will Jesus still continue with him as his guest? Zacchaeus, not Jesus, speaks next. Was Zacchaeus – who has also stopped and stood in the midst of all these prying eyes having been accused of being a sinner – wondering if this was the end of his elation? Was he wondering if the man from Galilee would agree with their assessment? Was he doing his own self-evaluation of his sin, value and worth? It is unclear and the text doesn't reveal all that went through this pint-sized guy's mind, but we see he speaks first and his first comments are directed to Jesus and not the crowd. He speaks in defense of Jesus' choice to be his guest.

"The half of my goods I give to the poor," Zacchaeus said. The Owner never stops him, corrects him, or rebukes him as a liar. Now understand, Jesus called him by name, Jesus knows who he is, Jesus would have known if his statement were true. Jesus says nothing.

Then I believe Zacchaeus directs his next part of his response towards the crowd of "Jerichoians" who had grumbled and accused him and Jesus.

Zacchaeus said to the crowd, "And if I have defrauded anyone of anything, I restore it fourfold." With Jesus, his Owner, not correcting his assertion concerning half his goods being given to the poor, he then directs his attention to the crowd of grumblers laying down a gauntlet for any who dare to take it up. Zacchaeus not only declared himself free of his accuser's grumbles, but offers to right the wrong if any of the onlookers can articulated proof of his corruption. Not a person in the large crowd takes him up on his offer. What a guy! In that one statement, Zacchaeus vindicated himself and Jesus' choice of him to be a guest at his home.

Here are my two huge takeaways at this juncture. Zacchaeus was giving away half of his goods and was still rich, a notable fact the writer includes in the text.

He had integrity in his business dealings and was not defrauding or cheating anyone in a business known for cunning dealings. One more thing, he had a house; he had ownership of property!

Let's look at what transpired next while the people of Jericho and the traveling crowd are both still captive audiences. Now Jesus begins to speak. Realize all are waiting to hear what the Man who is the cause of all this commotion and city uproar will say. Well, here it is,

"And Jesus said to him, *"Today salvation has come to this house, since he also is a son of Abraham."*

Jesus actually addresses both Zacchaeus and the crowd. Jesus makes a declaration He made to no other person in His thirty-three plus years on the earth. He makes a declaration not made in scripture to this point. Jesus tells Zacchaeus "today (not after I give my life for you, not after I am raised from the dead, not after you believe in me according to the law and commandments, not after anything) salvation has come to this house."

Why this guy? What is it about him that brings about such a declaration? If you took a look back at Luke 18:26 as Jesus is talking to another rich man about eternal life, the disciples ask him a question.

> 26 *"Those who heard it said,*
> *Then who can be saved?"*
>
> *- Luke 18:26*

My answer is Zacchaeus! Within twenty-four hours of another rich guy missing salvation because he lacked one thing, here is a living example of another rich guy, who gets what less than a day before was considered impossible. Here is Jesus' response to the above question.

> 27 *"What is impossible with man*
> *is possible with God."*
>
> *- Luke 18:27*

A rich person getting in the kingdom of God is what was considered to be impossible. But only twenty-four hours later, we have a rich guy receiving salvation! The conclusion of the declaration to Zacchaeus is just as telling as "salvation coming to his house." "Since he also is a son of Abraham." Abraham was the patriarch, the father of all the Jewish people. He was the one of whom all Jews identified. He was the father of promise. The father of faith. The friend of God. Abraham is one of the best examples of a human being on earth receiving promises from God before the expected time. Jesus declares Zacchaeus a son of Abraham, a son of promise, a son of faith, a son who is a friend of God (Jesus is having lunch with him), and one who is receiving a promise before its expected availability. This promise is activated by an action of faith so spectacular God allows that which shouldn't be allowed. Abraham believed God and it was counted to him as righteousness (Romans 4:3), though Jesus had not yet brought us righteousness. Zacchaeus tapped into salvation before salvation was made available through the death, burial, and resurrection of Christ. Everyone standing there would have understood this reference.

Now this is where it gets interesting, Jesus has just said salvation belongs to Zacchaeus. It had to already be a done deal, because Jesus was headed to his house, he had specifically called him by name. Jesus said, "I must stay at your house today." So obviously, Jesus' next statement is not directed at Zacchaeus.

> [10] "For the Son of Man came to
> seek and to save the lost."
>
> - Luke 19:10

I believe this was directed at the crowd. If you read the account from start to finish, who would appear lost in the unfolding of the story? Perhaps not those traveling with Jesus, but surely the grumblers. They need to not only learn from Zacchaeus, they should aspire to be like him. The writer and the text make a clear distinction about Zacchaeus; he was rich! But Jesus went to his house, called him a son of Abraham, and said salvation has come to his entire house. Does this sound like God has a problem with us being rich? I submit to you; the answer is no! Jesus left everyone standing in the street for this guy. May we be so fortunate to become rich like Zacchaeus!

I will not take time to totally unpack in this book the parable that Jesus launches into immediately after the Zacchaeus encounter. But imagine, while all the crowd from Galilee and the hordes on the streets of Jericho are still standing there in shock at what had transpired, Jesus introduces a familiar parable about the minas or talents (depending on the book of the Bible and translation of the Bible). It is a continuation of all that just occurred.

If you want to get a full rundown on this parable, then you can order the companion book to this one, *Champions of Justice*. I'm aware I've referenced my book a few times, but it is the foundation of what I teach on the subject of justice. It can give you a little taste of what to expect! Now back to the point at hand.

With the captive crowd dumbfounded, Jesus begins telling a parable of a nobleman who went off into a far country to receive a kingdom and return. While He was away, He gave minas/talents (money) to His servants left behind and told them to occupy (do business) until He returned. After some time, He returned and had two questions for His servants.

1. "What did you do with the money I gave you?"

2. "What did you do to improve the business I left with you?"

These are the same two questions that were answered by Zacchaeus. I believe the parable of the talents was a perfect depiction, a case study, for anyone who would be a Zacchaeus type. The parable unlocks the hidden mysteries of the life of Zacchaeus who just stunned the crowd. My book will give you much more. You are welcome to investigate my website located in the back of this booklet.

THE PATH OF JUSTICE

CHAPTER FIVE
WHY BE RICH?

I agree, the interaction of Jesus with Zacchaeus along with the parable of the talents was a climatic culmination of a two-and-a-half-week journey of Jesus and His entourage from Galilee to Jerusalem. Jericho was His final city before His triumphant entry, betrayal, crucifixion, death, and resurrection. The first parable Jesus gives on this journey is the prelude to the story of Zacchaeus separated by a sequence of events culminated on the streets of Jericho. I flesh this out in another one of my companion books titled *Streets of Justice*. I will give you this small excerpt to help you see why Jesus may have paid attention to this Zacchaeus type. The following passage is a short read from *Streets of Justice*.

> None of us have the luxury of waiting on others to do justice. We have to be like the "Good Samaritan" in Luke chapter 10 who acted immediately to help a stranger even when others had chosen not to. In Luke 10:25, a lawyer asks Jesus, "what must I do to gain eternal life?" At the end of a lengthy discourse, Jesus told the lawyer, "you go do likewise."

> Like many of us, this guy wanted to know what he must do to get to heaven, to see the next life, to gain passage to what he felt would be next.

> Keeping the commandments was the first thing, which the lawyer assured Jesus he was doing. Next, the lawyer said it was required to love God with all your heart, soul, mind and strength, which he was also doing. But then came this little statement, "love your neighbor as yourself." The lawyer then asked Jesus, "who is my neighbor?"

The rest of the story was a parable with four characters. All of the individuals were on a road between the city of Jerusalem and a town called Jericho. The first man on the road fell prey to thieves who robbed, beat, and left him for dead.

Next is a priest who comes down the road and sees the helpless injured man and moves quickly past on the other side of the road. Priests are considered those who represent God on earth.

Then a Levite comes by and he also passes by and continues without offering any assistance to the man who was robbed. Levites are those who are servants of God known for their sacrifice as helpers.

Last, a Samaritan on a journey sees the injured man and comes to his aide. He bandages his wounds, puts him on his donkey and takes him to an inn. He cares for him until he has to leave. He then leaves funds with the inn keeper to continue the man's care until he's well, conveying if any additional cost is incurred, he, the Samaritan, would pay the bill on his next journey.

Jesus asks the lawyer, "who do you think was the neighbor?"

"The Samaritan," the lawyer says. Jesus having depicted an undeniable conclusion said, "you go do likewise." Though the care shown by the Samaritan is a tremendous example of being a neighbor. It has a more profound implication. You see, the Samaritan and the injured man (a Jew) are not neighbors; they are enemies. The Jews call the Samaritans dogs. Jesus is saying you go be that kind of "dog" to someone else!

Doing justice does not distinguish culture, color, creed, or cause; it can't afford to.

Four people were going down the road, either could
have been five minutes earlier and ended up being
the injured man. As long as we all "do likewise," it
shouldn't matter. But if we aren't doing likewise, how
can you safely walk down any road?

"Love your neighbor as yourself." The conversation
between Jesus and the lawyer concluded with the
thought that to have eternal life, an individual has to
resemble, model, and exemplify the term neighbor.

"Neighbor" launched a clarification parable with
staggering implications. The conclusion? If you want
eternal life, then, "go do likewise!"

Being the "Samaritan type of neighbor"
demonstrated the essence of both eternal life and
true love. The Samaritan willingly used his capability
and means to put things right for another;
he was just!

Hosea says, "return." Return from what? Your lack of
justice and love shown to others!
- Author Steffron James

Did you see the similarities? These guys were doing business in
an honorable way but willingly using their capabilities and means
to put things right for others in a just way. This brought salvation
for Zacchaeus and his entire house and it was eternal life and the
essence of love shown by a Samaritan to a lawyer needing to know
what he must do to secure life. Be a Zacchaeus or Samaritan kind
of neighbor. "Go do likewise!"

By the way, did you notice both stories referenced Jericho? Luke, the
writer of this book, ties the two parables together. The word Jericho
means *place of fragrance.* When we are a "do likewise neighbor," we
create a wonderful fragrance for others, no matter where they are!

Now here is my question to you the reader of this book: "Do the
callouts/observations I have given give cause to take another look at
this guy and what we've explored? I truly hope so; it's sure worth it!

I have spent the last five chapters hopefully getting you to see God has no issue with our being rich, wealthy, prosperous, or having abundance. But the pink elephant still throughout those chapters is "why be rich?"

Why should you want to be wealthy? That's one of the main reasons for my writing this book. Riches and wealth better position us to put things right for others. Means, resources, and capital can be used to eradicate injustice in many ways. When we have justice dictated as a core value and we are vigilantly mindful of our assignment to be doing likewise, we become the embodiment, the exemplification and the personification of all things justice.

Zacchaeus gave half of his goods to the poor. What would possess a man to have such a conviction of cause and yielding of self-preservation and self-indulgence? I submit for your consideration: he, like the servant with the minas/talents (money), recognized his ability to use what the Lord had given him as a means of increase, was not for himself, but for his owner. He discovered the key was water and you will be watered. He realized he that brings blessings will be enriched. He now gets it; he that gives freely will grow all the richer. He's concluded, he that works his land will have plenty of bread. It is now known to him, in all labor there is profit. His now resounding confession is, "it is God that gives power to get wealth to fulfill His covenant."

Zacchaeus as a son of Abraham had the promise and mandate of Abraham; "you are blessed to be a blessing to others." What wealth brings to you is generally not for you but to pass through you. Can God pass resources through you without them sticking to you and being consumed upon your own lust?

....

IF GOD CAN TRUST YOU WITH HIS MINAS/TALENTS [MONEY] TO BRING HIM A RETURN ON HIS INVESTMENT, THEN YOU NEVER HAVE TO WORRY ABOUT HIS REWARD TO YOU.

....

I want to introduce you to a concept that I believe is the reason for your wealth, riches, increase, and abundance. It is a thing called justice. I know you think you have heard about it before, but hang in there with me, I am sure you'll learn at least one nugget that can help you understand it better.

What does all this have to do with justice? Everything! The wealth of the wicked is laid up for the just. But the just have to be just to receive it or else it might as well stay with the wicked so God does not have to judge us for misappropriation of His funds.

In the parable of the talents, He called the guy who had no return on His investment a wicked and slothful servant. I define justice as *"willingly using your capability and means to put things right for others.* Capability deals with your position, capacity, skill, intellect, energy, wits, influence and any other ability at your disposal. Means deals with capital, resources, money, land, property, investments, etc. Means give purchasing power. If any of us use our capability and means to put things right for others in a just way, then we are doers of justice. The mystery is when God finds people who have this as an operating principle, He brings resources their way to fulfill His plans on the earth. Let me show you what I mean by exploring a couple of scriptures.

> [20] *"I walk in the way of righteousness, in the paths of justice,* [21] *granting an inheritance to those who love me, and filling their treasuries."*
>
> *- Proverbs 8:20-21*

In this verse, God is speaking. He indicates He walks in the way of righteousness; no one should have a problem agreeing with God on that assertion. It is God speaking and of course He is righteous. But he is also walking on the paths of justice. Notice the text says paths with an "s". What is He doing on the *Paths of Justice?* "Granting an inheritance to those who love him and filling their treasuries."

I don't know about you, but this verse makes me want to find the justice path. It is on that path you meet God and it is on that path He meets you with your inheritance and what it will take to fill your "treasuriessssss." (Ok, I made up this word but you get the point;

45

that means more than one.) Your treasures are for His justice to be accomplished in the earth. The word "filling" has attached to it a continuation of an action as often as needed. Another word used in the definition for filling is replenishing. God replenishes your treasures as you do justice on His behalf! What a tremendous promise!

Try out this next one:

> *⁵ "It is well with the man who deals generously and lends; who conducts his affairs with justice."*
>
> *- Psalm 112:5*

"It is well." This statement is loaded! When someone in the Old Testament said it was well, that meant *every area of their life was good,* nothing out of order, nothing damaged, nothing having issues. It would be like going to the doctor and getting a clean bill of health. He notifies you, "all is well!" That is celebration time! Well is well! Well is the hope and desire of all! Well is contentment and peace of mind that all things are right in the world! What man gets to be a partaker of this "wellness?" The one who deals generously and lends, who conducts his affairs with justice. Yes! It is well with him or her who deals generously and lends!

I think these two points are the same just said in a different way. If you deal generously and lend, you are conducting your affairs with justice. Remember our scripture from the opening chapter, *"He that lends to the poor lends to the Lord and the Lord will repay him."* (Proverbs 19:17) What will the Lord repay him? According to this scripture, wellness. And according to our previous verse above, replenished treasures. Are you even considering justice as you do your affairs? You are now, right?

Before I inundate you with scriptures tying wealth and riches to justice, let me give you God's perspective on justice.

> *"But the LORD sits enthroned forever; he has established his throne for justice."*
>
> *- Psalm 9:7*

> [4] *"The Rock, his work is perfect, for all his ways are justice. A God of faithfulness and without iniquity, just and upright is He."*
>
> *- Deuteronomy 32:4*

> [14] *"Righteousness and justice are the foundation of your throne; steadfast love and faithfulness go before you."*
>
> *- Psalm 89:14*

> [6] *"But the LORD of hosts is exalted in justice, and the Holy God shows himself holy in righteousness."*
>
> *- Isaiah 5:16*

> [18] *"Therefore the LORD waits to be gracious to you, and therefore he exalts himself to show mercy to you. For the LORD is a God of justice; **blessed** are all those who wait for him."*
>
> *- Isaiah 30:18*

I could keep going. My two previous books go into much more detail. This is just the tip of the iceberg of what God has to say about justice. But let me give you just one additional verse God indicates is a part of our justice assignment.

> [2] *"Who can utter the mighty deeds of the LORD, or declare all his praise?* [3] ***Blessed** are they who observe justice, who do righteousness at all times!"*
>
> *- Psalm 106:2-3*

The last two verses highlighted both have the word "blessed." I bolded both for you. Blessed means full supply, having absolutely everything needed to function at maximum capacity. Blessed is a result of waiting for the God of justice or observing justice (doing justice) and righteousness at all times.

Are you observing justice? Are you even justice conscious? The Lord's deeds and praise according to verse two are connected to the act of justice. Giving God the praise and reverence due to him falls short without justice and righteousness being in play in your life.

Let me share the continuation of the thought of the writer of Isaiah 30:18. Here is the last line of verse eighteen. *"For the LORD is a God of justice; **blessed** are all those who wait for him."* Verses nineteen through twenty-one are the promises for the **"blessed"** who wait for the God of justice.

Verses 19-21 say, *"For a people shall dwell in Zion (the Church), in Jerusalem (any city); you shall weep no more. He (God) will surely be gracious to you at the sound of your cry. As soon as God hears it (your cry), He (God) answers you. 20 And though the Lord give you the bread of adversity and the water of affliction, yet your Teacher will not hide himself anymore, but your eyes shall see your Teacher. 21 And your ears shall hear a word behind you, saying, **"this is the way, walk in it**," when you turn to the right or when you turn to the left."*

Those who know, do, execute, and administer justice will be on the path of God and will hear a Word saying, *"This is the way of **justice**; walk in it."* For justice is the way of God. Let's continue on...

This next one is a little longer, but well worth the read. The blessings, treasures, and being well is wonderful, but we also need protection from the things that can rob us of our blessings, wealth, treasures, and well-being.

> 6 *"For the Lord gives wisdom; from his mouth come knowledge and understanding;* 7 *he stores up sound wisdom for the upright; he is a shield to those who walk in integrity,* 8 *guarding the paths of justice and watching over the way of his saints.* 9 *Then you will understand righteousness and justice and equity, every good path;"*
>
> - Proverbs 2:6-9

Proverbs 2:6 says, "*The Lord gives wisdom.*" What is in the left hand of wisdom? Riches and honor (Proverbs 3:16). But I want to really draw your attention to Proverbs 2:8 when the scripture says, *"guarding the paths of justice."* If you are observing justice, doing justice, being just, then God Himself is guarding you. He is a shield to you. He is your protector as you do your acts of justice. When you gain the wisdom of walking in the paths of justice verse nine says, "then you will understand righteousness, justice, and equity, every good path. With justice as your guide, you'll stop venturing down the wrong paths. You will know and see good paths for your life. I submit to you justice is a good path, with benefits.

> [5] *"The Lord is exalted, for he dwells on high;*
> *he will fill Zion with justice and righteousness,*
> [6] *and he will be the stability of your times,*
> *abundance of salvation, wisdom, and knowledge;*
> *the fear of the Lord is Zion's treasure."*
>
> *- Isaiah 33:5-6*

Isaiah 33:5-6 articulates a tremendous promise to Zion, the church. This verse starts with exalting the Lord and declaring His majestic position as the highest of heights. Then comes the promises. He, this exalted Lord, Owner, and Champion of the Universe gives promises to His people. The first promise, *"He will fill Zion with justice and righteousness."* He will fill. This means Zion (the church) will be packed full, overflowing, and stuffed to capacity with justice and righteousness.

Here comes the next statement, *"and he will be the stability of your times."* Notice he doesn't distinguish the time that He stabilizes. Whenever justice and righteousness show up, then stability comes with them to bring a firmness to your situation, circumstances, tribulation, upheaval, pain, dysfunction and confusion. Stability helps us see clearly. It helps us get past the turbulence of our time.

The other result of stability is peace! When justice and righteousness fill Zion, "abundance of salvation, wisdom, and knowledge" are the by-products. Abundance of all of these happens as a result of Zion being filled with justice and righteousness. We could take time to break down each word, but that's your homework! For the sake of time, let's just say if you could have abundance of salvation, wisdom, and knowledge, would that benefit your life? It flows out of justice.

THE PATH OF JUSTICE

CHAPTER SIX
THE "YOU" APPLICATION

I hope you have noticed though justice and righteousness are partnered in many of these scriptures, in most cases justice is listed first. Though they are both vital and necessary, they have very unique and distinctive characteristics. Finally, "the fear of the Lord is Zion's treasure." A reverence for the Lord of justice becomes your treasure. There is that word treasure again.

> ⁷ *"But we have this treasure in jars of clay,*
> *to show that the surpassing power belongs*
> *to God and not to us."*
>
> *- 2 Corinthians 4:7*

When we operate in and for justice, the treasure within us demonstrates the power of God. Justice brings God's greatness in and through us. Let me wrap up this section with a verse that I will not give a commentary on. Let it speak to you by itself.

> ¹ *"Behold my servant, whom I uphold, my chosen,*
> *in whom my soul delights; I have put my Spirit upon*
> *him; he will bring forth justice to the nations.* ² *He*
> *will not cry aloud or lift up his voice, or make it heard*
> *in the street;* ³ *a bruised reed he will not break, and*
> *a faintly burning wick he will not quench; he will*
> *faithfully bring forth justice.* ⁴ *He will not grow faint or*
> *be discouraged till he has established justice in the*
> *earth; and the coastlands wait for his law."*
>
> *- Isaiah 42:1-4 (ESV)*

Okay, just a little summary. The chosen servant in whom the Lord delights, who He puts His Spirit upon, this individual brings justice to every people group. He won't make a racket in the streets; he won't oppress others or be a detriment to anyone else's purpose.

He will focus and give attention to faithfully bringing forth justice. Regardless of what happens, this person will not get tired, quit, or become discouraged until he has established justice in the earth. From coast to coast, people will be waiting for this type of person to show up. I think that is a pretty good Steffron summary of this verse! Of course, this is a picture of Jesus. But as you go through this next collage of scriptures, you will hopefully began to see there is a Jesus application and a "You" application.

> [17] *"learn to do good; seek justice, correct oppression; bring justice to the fatherless, plead the widow's cause."*
>
> *- Isaiah 1:17 (ESV)*

> [4] *"Give attention to me, my people, and give ear to me my nation; for the law will go out from me, and I will set my justice for a light to the people."* *(nations-every people group)*
>
> *- Isaiah 51:4 (ESV)*

> [1] *"Thus says the LORD: "Keep justice, and do righteousness, for soon my salvation will come, and my righteousness be revealed."*
>
> *- Isaiah 56:1 (ESV)*

> [9] *"Thus says the LORD of hosts: '***execute** *true justice, show mercy and compassion Everyone to his brother."*
>
> *- Zechariah 7:9 (NKJV)*

Do you see what I mean by the "You" application? These are written for our learning and appropriation.

I want to bring this to a close by going to the New Testament and capturing a small portion of the life of the Apostle Paul especially towards the end of his life. Please come with me to the book of Acts where the author Luke reveals some things about Paul I missed for years. We will start in chapter eighteen. Let me get you up to speed.

The Apostle Paul – who had persecuted the church as a zealous young radical – had a powerful conversion and became a follower and proclaimer of the One he had previously denounced. The converted Paul was sent out from a base church in Antioch where he became a traveling minister to the unchurched Gentile population of various regions and towns. He visited places like Pisidia, Iconium, Derbe, Lystra, Philippi, Thessalonica, Athens, and finally Corinthians and Ephesus. The crazy thing was he got ran out, beat, stoned, and persecuted in almost every town he entered until he came to Corinth. Paul was a phenomenal orator. He was a real preacher and apostle. But wherever he went there were riots and uprising. Let's pick up his story in Acts 18.

> [1] *"After this Paul left Athens and went to Corinth.*
> [2] *And he found a Jew named Aquila, a native of*
> *Pontus, recently come from Italy with his wife*
> *Priscilla, because Claudius had commanded all*
> *the Jews to leave Rome. And he went to see*
> *them,* [3] *and because he was of the same trade,*
> *he stayed with them and worked, for they*
> *were tentmakers by trade."*
>
> *- Acts 18:1-3 (ESV)*

The preacher became a worker. Guess what? This is the first town he didn't get run out of! When there was an uprising, Paul was about to speak, but in verse fourteen others defended him and he was able to continue for some time without any more upheaval. Paul stayed in Corinth a minimum of eighteen months, but it could have been longer. Then he decided to leave of his own volition, without being run out of town, to go on to Asia to a town called Ephesus in particular. But there is one thing that he did that is clearly detailed in the account of his leaving Corinth.

Acts 18:18 tells us, *"After this, Paul stayed many days longer and then took leave of the brothers and set sail for Syria, **and with him Priscilla and Aquila**. At Cenchreae he had cut his hair, for he was under a vow."*

Did you catch that? As he left this city (which for the first time he didn't get chased out), he took with him Priscilla and Aquila. What has Paul discovered? Why did joining with Pricilla and Aquila and making tents open a door that had not previously been open? Why did it give him influence not ever afforded? And why now were others defending this guy?

The text doesn't give the backdrop, but something is very different. After Corinth, Paul takes some time away to have a secluded time with a vow he'd made. Was he pondering, considering, contemplating for himself what was so different? I can only speculate. However, when we return to Ephesus where he left his working partners Priscilla and Aquila, he enters the synagogue with twelve disciples. After three months of trying to get the people to listen to no avail, Paul leaves the synagogue with the disciples and goes next door to a hall, school, or training area. If you catch the timing, he didn't get run out, he changed where he was trying to reach people. The scripture reference for this is Acts 19: 9.

> [9] *"But when some became stubborn and continued in unbelief, speaking evil of the Way before the congregation, he withdrew from them and took the disciples with him, reasoning daily in the hall of Tyrannus."*
>
> *- Acts 19:9 (ESV)*

What happens next is staggering to think about especially when we know Paul has never had a chance to make a long-term, significant impact because he is run out of town before he can make a huge difference. I am not saying Paul didn't accomplish a great deal. But what he accomplished in Ephesus and Asia were unparallel to any other city he visited. Some historical accounts say over half the city turned to Christ.

Check out the next verse:

> [10] *"This continued for two years, so that all the residents of Asia heard the word of the Lord, both Jews and Greeks."*
>
> *- Acts 19:10 (ESV)*

Paul was in Ephesus for two years. He didn't get run out of town and there was no uprising! (Acts 19:30-31) But here is the spectacular occurrence. In just two years, "**ALL**" the residents of Asia heard the word of the Lord, both Jews and Greeks. After Paul begins to work in the marketplace, interacting with people on a daily basis, has a valued skill, a marketable trade, works his land, and as you will see in another couple of paragraphs begins to supply to others out of his capability and means, everything changes for him. What did this mighty apostle learn at the later parts of his ministry? Justice is no respecter of persons. It is not partial, but it is blind. What is different about what Paul is doing? Who's in his life and what difference is it making? The only thing the scriptures show that has change is this couple, Pricilla and Aquila, are now a part of the staff.

JUSTICE IS NO RESPECTER OF PERSONS. IT IS NOT PARTIAL, BUT IT IS BLIND.

Down below I give you a couple of other items, but for now these two standout. His work partners were the ones Paul made sure he had with him when he proceeded to his next town. These two tent makers had taken aside the skilled, eloquent, and powerful orator of the scriptures Apollos and taught even him a better way of being impactful. *See Acts 18:26.*

After over three years in Ephesus, there is finally somewhat of an uprising, but the Asiarchs (the chief people of the region), Paul's friends advise him to stay away and again Paul is defended by others. Why is this significant? At no other time is Paul said to have friends outside of ministry partners like a guy named Barnabas. Paul has begun to work, build relationship, invest in his community, give back to others, supply to others, and build partnerships. We often overlook the need for others when we are attempting to fulfill the plan of God for our lives.

When I moved to Tennessee with a wife and five children not knowing anyone in Tennessee, I knew I had a call on my life. But I also had mouths to feed and the responsibility as a man to care for what God had entrusted to my stewardship. Start a ministry, start a job, elicit support, start a small group or just trust God to supply;

these were all questions I asked myself? Through a sequence of events I ended up deciding to do real estate sales.

Mind you, it was a profession I had never explored. Get this; when you first become a real estate agent your survival may depend on your sphere of influence to get you off the ground. You hit up family, friends, acquaintances, and people you have come to know in your community. Big problem, I knew no one except the guy who sold me my house and asked me to join his real estate team. Next big problem, he couldn't pay me a salary so it would be a full commission job with no safety net.

Well, that was sure not in the plan. But after seeking God and long talks with my wife and every counsel I could get, I went for it. Was it scary? You betcha! I remember times I closed my office door, wrote "sold" across houses that were on the market and began declaring they would get buyers because the mortgage, utilities, food, kids, needs, vehicle repairs and the like didn't stop arriving just because I made a "faith move." Much like Paul, I would fast, pray, confess scriptures, sacrifice, and work with all I knew how. But hindsight has shown me, though those things were vital and wonderful to include in any endeavor, you can do them and still fail miserably.

My first year in real estate, I did twenty-five transactions. My second year I did fifty. Anyone who has ever ventured into real estate knows the average agent does less than five transactions per year. My family would have starved.

Six months after starting real estate, we launched a ministry. Within two years, we were bursting at the seams of the small space we were occupying in a meeting room at the building where my real estate office was located. Here's the amazing part of the two years. Probably seventy five percent of the people who joined the church were people I had met in real estate. I had sold them a house, worked with them on a deal, went to them for a mortgage, or just come across their path as I did my daily business.

Paul reached all of Asia within two years, but only after he started working with Pricilla and Aquila. In the twelve years I pastored, I always kept my real estate job. It allowed me to grow the ministry, help fund the ministry, be one of the largest givers in the ministry, sow into helping others, to be a justice advocate even when I didn't know what it was. This is not a boast in any way, but in twelve years of ministry, I never took a salary. Not because it wasn't offered or I thought it was wrong. I just decided I would trust God and be an example to the people. Some have said to me, "you robbed your people of being a blessing and receiving a blessing."

My reply was always, "I always encouraged tithing, offerings, giving to the poor, and supporting endeavors God speaks to your hearts...but do it to "the least of these." (Matthew 25:45) If people give to what Jesus said to give to, if I am the example of what Jesus said to give to, then the people and I get blessed as we partner in our obedience. I am not building a doctrine. I am communicating observations from Luke's account of Paul's life and my own personal journey. My people were tremendously blessed and I was blessed because money and truth were never an issue between me and the people. They never wondered if it was about the money for me.

One more little testimony about the people. In twelve years of ministry we never took up an offering on Sunday morning for the church. A box was in the back and they gave as directed by the Holy Spirit. Not one hundred percent, but most of my people were tithers, givers, and suppliers and didn't have to be arm twisted or guilted into it. Faith is faith for every area of your life. When we teach people to believe God, read and study the Word for themselves, they operate in faith in every area of life, tithing and giving included.

Why do I tell you about my experience at my church startup? My best friends and those who have been a tremendous blessing to me all came from my joining a real estate team with a guy who I still work with today. This guy was the first member of my startup church. This guy, outside of God, has been the single most impactful relationship I have had in my adult life outside of my wife. Only one person supplied more to the ministry than me. It was him. He has been and is a friend. He is still a business partner. He's my Pricilla and Aquila.

Who are these tentmakers? And how is it that Paul's connection with them has suddenly made him effective and even Apollos receives instruction from this couple? The chief people of Asia are his friends, when every other place he's been, Paul is number one on the most-wanted list. Also did you notice the writer, Luke, has no problem mentioning Priscilla's name first in several passages. It is believed she was the more vocal and prominent between she and her husband. She was possibly the front office customer service (or the CEO!) person and her husband Aquila was the hands-on, back-in-the-warehouse guy, so to speak.

But this was the way it seemed to operate in their ministering to others also. Priscilla appears to be a business woman who had a role in establishing the early church.

What's my point? Don't be afraid of building relationships as believers to advance the kingdom of God in business. Your spirituality does not eliminate practicality. Business is a kingdom concept. Luke 19:10 referring to Jesus as the nobleman says, *"engage in business until I come."*

What transpired for me in my twelve years of ministry, I didn't find in a handbook and I don't suggest it's the only way. But when I look at what happened with Paul and consider the impact he had, I think I am in good company. Let me show you what I am referring to.

We don't get to truly see or know all that transpired with Paul until he's concluding his time in Asia. Then we get a little peek at what has happened to and with him. As he is departing for Jerusalem, he calls for the Ephesians' Elders to meet him to have a farewell time on a beach just as he's about to board a ship. Paul does a powerful benediction with these elders. But then he talks about his three years at Ephesus. I want to cover these few verses for our purposes of this book. (Acts 20:31-37)

There is a huge amount here. I will pull out what has bearing on our subject matter. Paul says in Acts 20:33, "*I coveted no one's silver or gold or apparel.*" That is a good statement and I would hope he hadn't. But the next statement is what sets Paul apart from the preacher who got ran out of town in the first part of his ministry and is now reaching their entire region in just two years.

> [34] *"You yourselves know that these hands ministered to my necessities and to those who were with me"*
>
> *- Acts 20:34 (ESV)*

The preacher has worked with his hands and taken care of his necessities and those who were with him. Paul is a worker and carer for others. Sounds like Zacchaeus and the Samaritan to me. Paul the tent maker is a marketplace guy who is willingly using his capability and means to put things right for others in a just way for the just One. Paul's performing of justice has led him to reaching all of Asia in two years. He tells them for three years, this is how I lived among you. Verse thirty-five really brings it home.

> [35] *"In all things I have shown you that by working hard in this way we must help the weak and remember the words of the Lord Jesus, how he himself said, 'It is more blessed to give than to receive."*
>
> *- Acts 20:35 (ESV)*

That is in your Bible! Remember, *"He that works his land will have plenty of bread."* (Proverbs 12:11) Paul has worked hard, he has showed the Ephesians how to be successful in ministry. It is amazing, in all my thirty-three plus years in the Lord and over thirty in some form of ministry, I have never heard a preacher use this verse to say I have worked hard with my hands to take care of all my own needs and the needs of those with me.

Thankfully, I have met people who I applaud whose lives exemplify this very conviction of Paul, but I have not heard it as a way of life preached. Paul said, "we (anyone in a leadership position as I am), must help the weak and remember the words of the Lord Jesus, how He Himself said, "It is more blessed to give than to receive."

We often hear those in leadership say, "it is more blessed to give than to receive" when encouraging parishioners to be givers. But I want to point out, Paul was saying this to a group of elders only. He was talking to the group he spent the most time with in Asia. He was talking to the group in the region where he had his most impactful ministry. Paul is telling these elders, when you are blessed, you can be a blessing. When you work with your hands you can be a blessing. When you are honorable in your business you can be a blessing. When you recognize the right business partnerships it is a blessing so you can be a blessing. In conclusion, I believe Acts 28 wraps it up for us!

> [30] *"He lived there two whole years at his own*
> *expense, and welcomed all who came to him,*
> [31] *proclaiming the kingdom of God and teaching*
> *about the Lord Jesus Christ with all*
> *boldness and without hindrance."*
>
> *- Acts 28:30-31 (ESV)*

Paul used **"his"** capability and means to willingly put things right for others in a just way for the Just One. I believe Paul was a Justice Champion in every description of the term. Paul shows all of us, you don't have to be rich, but there is not a problem with riches. Here's the more gargantuan issue; you have to be willing to use what you have for others.

Here's the last scripture I will leave you with as I close.

> [23] *"Thus says the LORD: "Let not the wise*
> *man boast in his wisdom, let not the mighty*
> *man boast in his might, let not the rich man boast*
> *in his riches,* [24] *but let him who boasts boast in this,*
> *that he understands and **knows me**, that I am the*
> *LORD who practices steadfast love, justice, and*
> *righteousness in the earth. For in these things*
> *I delight, declares the LORD."*
>
> *- Jeremiah 9:23-24*

Did you recognize wisdom, being mighty, and being rich are all seemingly noble and honorable admirations? But those are not the things that should be your confidence or place of pride. Here's what the Prophet Jeremiah tells us is a meaningful endeavor and worthy aspiration for each of us; "boast in this, that *you understand and know me,*" says God Himself. How is understanding and knowing Him measured? By grasping what He does and what brings Him (God) delight and joy. Here it is, "I am the LORD who practices steadfast love, justice, and righteousness in the earth. For in these things I delight, declares the LORD."

Jeremiah encourages us to make our boast about what God delights in and what ought to be in our thoughts. Can I challenge each of you? We have heard tremendous messages on the steadfast love of the Lord. We have received amazing teachings on appropriating the righteousness of God that only comes through Christ. But it seems we have neglected justice, especially justice as God intended. But that's now changing, right?

Remember the parable of the minas/talents(money)? Remember the first question of the nobleman, "what did you do with the money I gave you?" I am asking you, the reader of these pages, is justice even on your radar? Is there a consciousness about opportunities to right wrongs daily? Are your capabilities and means consumed upon you, yours, and no more? Are your affairs orchestrated to deal generously? Do you conduct your affairs with justice? Do you desire to be rich for the right reasons?

What if God's intention all along was for you to be rich in good works, to be ready to be generous, to be prepared for every good work? Riches aren't bad; they come with a need of responsible stewardship. Zacchaeus said, "half my goods I give to the poor." Jesus left all to spend the afternoon with him and salvation came to his house.

I pray this booklet has been helpful. But now it is up to you what you do with your Justice Mandate. My deepest desire is that these words have leaped off the page for your encouragement to see, understand, operate, do, execute, and advance justice in your sphere of influence. God is on the Paths of Justice!

ONE LAST QUESTION: ARE YOU?

Thank you for taking this journey with me;
for together, we are indeed

CHAMPIONS OF JUSTICE!

ABOUT THE AUTHOR
STEFFRON T. JAMES

Steffron T. James is a South Carolina native. He has made Tennessee his home for the past 17 years. He fondly refers to Tennessee as "the place where God lives." He served our country 22 1/2 years in the US Air Force. He enjoys real estate as his fun day job. Business development and entrepreneurship intrigue him, and he loves teaching and applying sound business practices in various aspects of life. Steffron's greatest passion is teaching the Word of God while challenging individuals to personal development and aspiring to their fullest potential. He is the author of Champions of Justice, the companion book to this one. His five children, three grandchildren, and a multitude of spiritual sons and daughters keep him young and enjoying life.

For more information visit: *www.thewayofjustice.com*

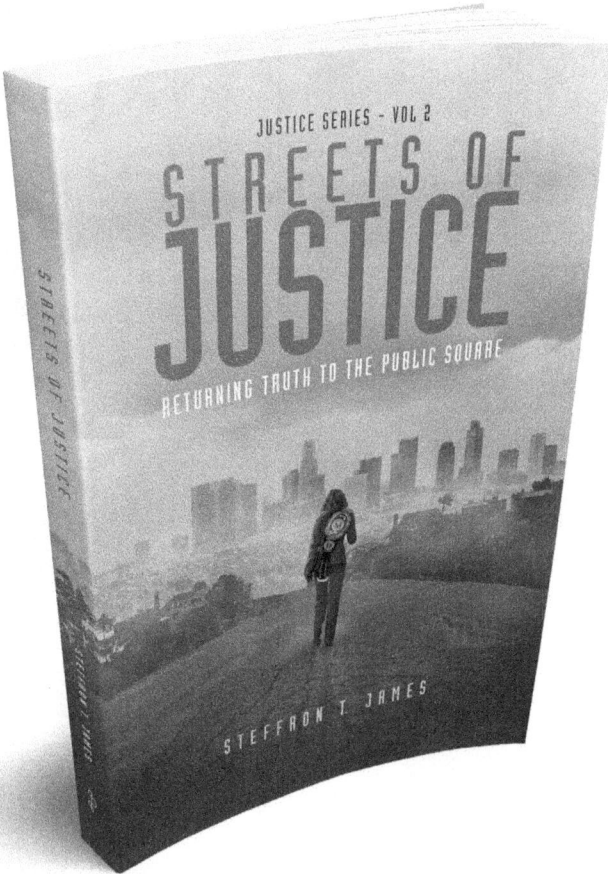

JUSTICE SERIES - VOL 4

THE WAY OF
JUSTICE

THE GAME CHANGER

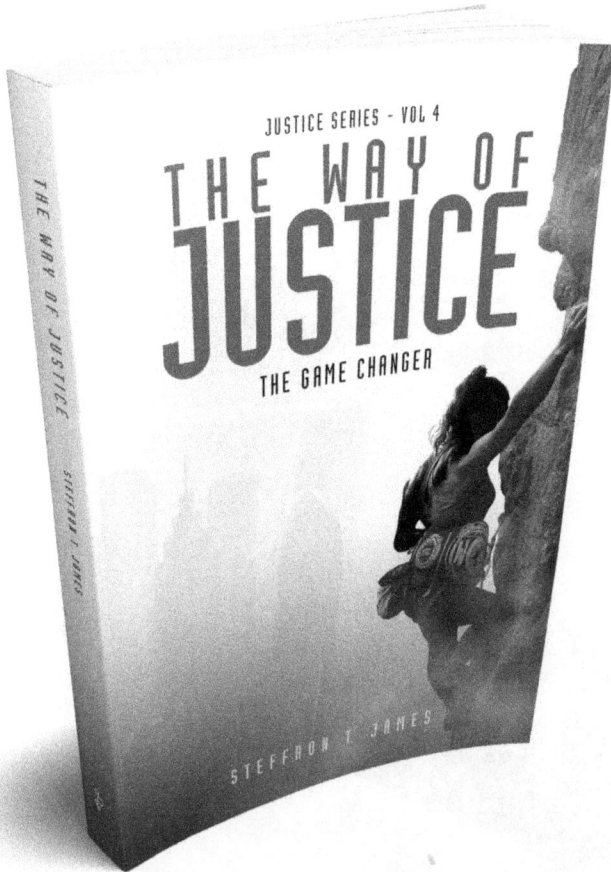

JUSTICE SERIES - VOL 4

THE WAY OF
JUSTICE

THE GAME CHANGER

STEFFRON T JAMES

Available at *www.thewayofjustice.com*

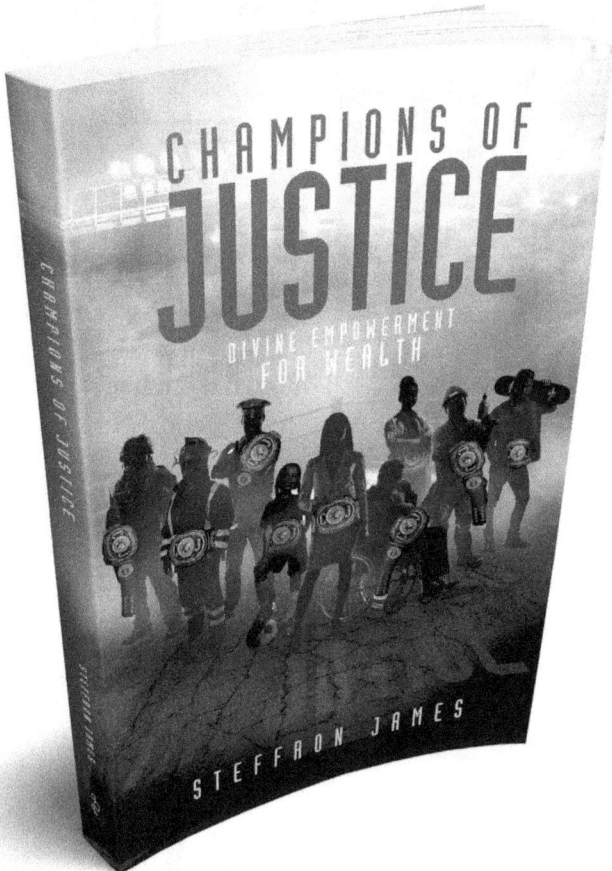

Available at *www.thewayofjustice.com*

JUSTICE SERIES - VOL 3

THE PATH OF
JUSTICE

TAPPING INTO YOUR TREASURES!

STEFFRON T. JAMES

www.ingramcontent.com/pod-product-compliance
Lightning Source LLC
Chambersburg PA
CBHW032208040426
42449CB00005B/498